SUSSEX
NARROW GAUGE

Vic Mitchell and Keith Smith

MP Middleton Press

Cover pictures:
Front upper - The Amberley Working Museum had the adjective added in 2001 to reflect its nature, not least in the field of industrial narrow gauge. Although built for a pleasure railway, the 2-4-0T Polar Bear *is a star attraction and was photographed on 5th July 1987 after a long overhaul. (P.Groom)*
Front lower - A minute passenger approaches the minimal train and its miniscule locomotive only five weeks before the last fare was collected on the Rye & Camber Tramway. (S.W.Baker)
Back upper - Volks Railway car 1 leaves Brighton's Aquarium station on 22nd May 1948, the driver using the unusual roof mounted controller. (J.H.Meredith)
Back lower - Authors Keith Smith (left) and Vic Mitchell squat beside no. 2 Northern Chief *at Hythe on 16th May 1999, prior to its departure with the 1.00pm book launch train for their* Romneyrail *album. (P.G.Barnes)*

Published July 2001

ISBN 1 901706 68 0

© *Middleton Press, 2001*

Design   Deborah Esher
Typesetting   Barbara Mitchell

Published by
            Middleton Press
            Easebourne Lane
            Midhurst, West Sussex
            GU29 9AZ
Tel: 01730 813169
Fax: 01730 812601

Printed & bound by Biddles Ltd,
            Guildford and Kings Lynn

CONTENTS

I.   Location of the railways included herein. All maps have north at the top and are to the scale of 25ins to 1 mile, unless otherwise stated. (D.H.Smith)

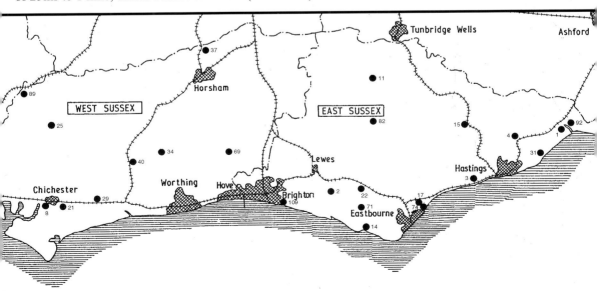

ACKNOWLEDGEMENTS

We record our gratitude to those mentioned in the credits and also to volunteers at the Amberley Working Museum, R.M.Casserley, G.Croughton, G.D.Coleman, A.D.Davies, I.Gledhill, B.Gooding, A.D.Heaver, Mr D. and Dr. S.Salter, P.Shaw, K.Webb and, as always, our ever supportive wives.

INTRODUCTION

There is great geological variety from south to north in Sussex, but remarkable uniformity east to west. Inland from the holidaymaker's "Sussex-by-the-Sea" there is a Gravel bearing coastal plain (West Sussex only), followed, in order, by the Chalk of the South Downs, Lower Greensand, Gault Clay, Upper Greensand and the great mass of Wealden Clay, plus an isolated pocket of Gypsum in East Sussex.

Most of these were worthy of exploitation and the narrow gauge railway was the economic answer to the local transport problem. Nothing now remains except in private collections or the Amberley Working Museum. We make no apology for giving much space to this important collection, which no stuudent of the subject can afford to miss seeing.

We have not included any of the numerous miniature railways in this volume and hope that sufficient illustrations are forthcoming to enable us to produce one devoted to the smaller gauges. Also omitted are private railways; there is a substantial 2ft 6ins gauge one hidden at Bolney.

Finally, we must refer readers to the classic *Industrial Railways of the South-East* (Middleton Press) for other views of many of the lines included in the first part of this book.

We hope you will enjoy our selection of Sussex narrow gauge lines.

Vic Mitchell
Keith Smith
May 2001

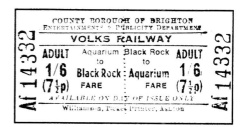

1. Industry

ABCO PETROLEUM - RYE

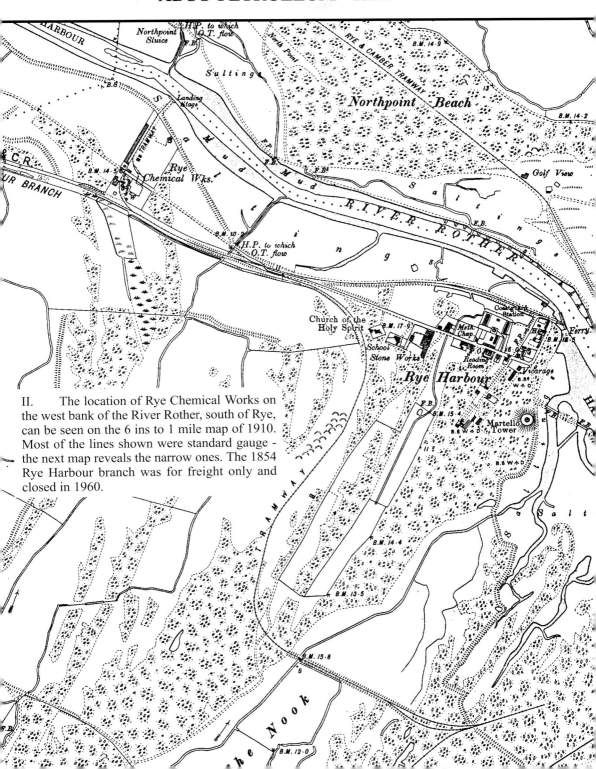

II.   The location of Rye Chemical Works on the west bank of the River Rother, south of Rye, can be seen on the 6 ins to 1 mile map of 1910. Most of the lines shown were standard gauge - the next map reveals the narrow ones. The 1854 Rye Harbour branch was for freight only and closed in 1960.

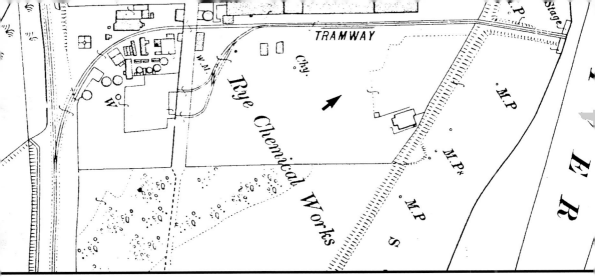

III.   The same edition at 25ins to 1 mile has mixed gauge track above the word TRAMWAY and 2 ft gauge ones running into the main part of the works. The premises have been used for tar, oil recovery, solvent reprocessing and petroleum products.

1.   A substantially rebuilt Ruston Hornsby diesel locomotive was recorded in April 1965. It was used for haulage of oil sludge at that time. Some of the track was on standard gauge sleepers to prevent it sinking on the sand walls of the sludge lagoons. The line, about 200yds long, was north of the road, not on the alignments shown on the map. (C.M.Jackson)

APCM - RODMELL WORKS

IV. The 1940 1ins to 1 mile map has been enlarged to show the short line which ends at the second **e** of **Cement Wks**. The halt is on the Seaford branch and was named Southease & Rodmell, the two villages being on the left of the map - the latter is uppermost.

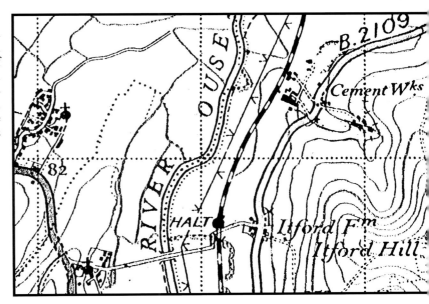

2. Associated Portland Cement operated several Ruston & Hornsby locomotives and they were recorded in June 1975, near the tipping shed, after their retirement and the line closed. There was a standard gauge siding (not shown on the map), but it was served by road vehicles from the works. (C.M.Jackson)

BAXTERS BRICKWORKS - BEXHILL

3.   The pit is two miles northwest of the centre of the town and was in use from 1888 to the present time. Since World War II, it has been operated in turn by M.P.Harris, Sussex & Dorking Brick Company, Redlands and Ibstock, recently being known as Ashdown Works. This 1962 view includes Motor Rail diesel no. 5292 of 1931, which was originally petrol. Rail operation ceased in about 1969, except in the drying sheds. The track was all of two-foot gauge. (C.G.Down)

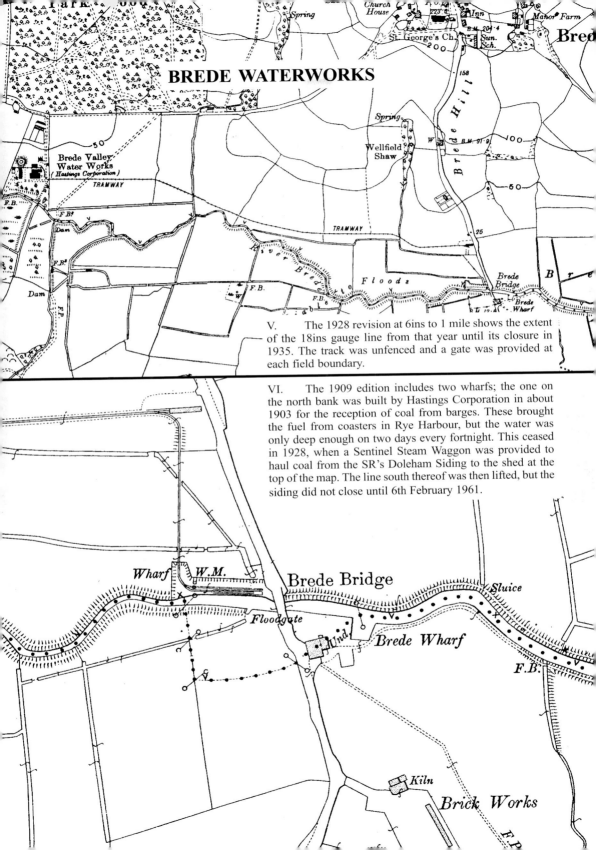

BREDE WATERWORKS

V.   The 1928 revision at 6ins to 1 mile shows the extent of the 18ins gauge line from that year until its closure in 1935. The track was unfenced and a gate was provided at each field boundary.

VI.   The 1909 edition includes two wharfs; the one on the north bank was built by Hastings Corporation in about 1903 for the reception of coal from barges. These brought the fuel from coasters in Rye Harbour, but the water was only deep enough on two days every fortnight. This ceased in 1928, when a Sentinel Steam Waggon was provided to haul coal from the SR's Doleham Siding to the shed at the top of the map. The line south thereof was then lifted, but the siding did not close until 6th February 1961.

4.   The railway was provided with this "Mercedes" class 0-4-0ST, which was built by Bagnall in 1899 as no. 1560. It was fitted with rectangular tanks in 1930, the boiler having been replaced in 1923. The bricks were conveyed for the construction of the works and lining of the three 10ft diameter wells, except for their upper 60ft which were lined with iron. (Hastings Library)

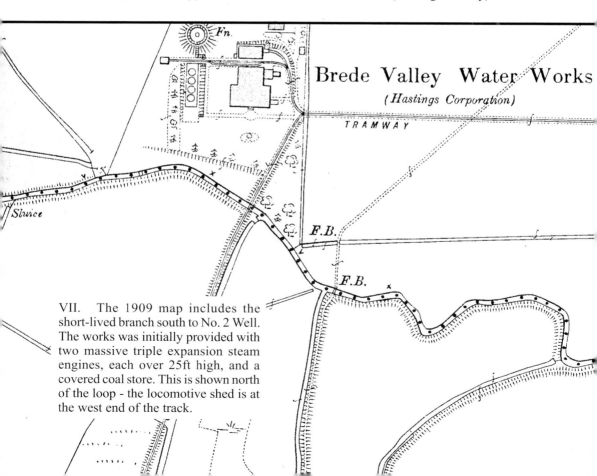

Fn.

Brede Valley Water Works

(Hastings Corporation)

T R A M W A Y

Sluice

F.B.

F.B.

VII.   The 1909 map includes the short-lived branch south to No. 2 Well. The works was initially provided with two massive triple expansion steam engines, each over 25ft high, and a covered coal store. This is shown north of the loop - the locomotive shed is at the west end of the track.

©R.C.Martin 1996

5.   The coal store had a hydraulic hoist at its east end, this lifting wagons up to roof level. They were emptied by shovel through hatches into five bunkers. The store capacity ws quoted as 500 tons, but calculations suggest only 200 tons. The building was demolished in 1939 to make way for another pumphouse. Some of the details are conjectural. (R.G.Martin)

6.   The barges were of 20 ton capacity and were unloaded with the help of this crane, which is astride the 18ins gauge track. Both are supported on timber piles. The Rye based *Victoria* was pictured in 1923 at the end of its eight mile journey. (P.A.L.Vine coll.)

◀——————

7.   The east elevation of the pumping engine house and the 99ft high chimney is seen, along with the track from the wharf, which turned in front of the building to reach the coal store. (P.A.L.Vine coll.)

CHICHESTER SEWAGE WORKS

8.   Haulage was undertaken by a diesel locomotive provided by Hibberd in 1936. It was one of a large batch of Simplex designs built by Motor Rail for use by the Army in World War I with petrol engines. After hostilities some 800 were bought by other manufacturers and re-engined. The shed contained an electric motor to start this one. (N.Palmer)

9.   The works was situated about one mile southwest of Chichester, at a site near Apuldram from which the purified water could drain into the channel that had earlier been used by the Romans to gain access to Fishbourne. The sludge train is seen in August 1976. (N.Palmer)

10.   The train is running past the sludge drying beds and in the background is the digester, which produced large volumes of methane. In some treatment works, this was used as fuel for transport. The locomotive and all the two-foot gauge track formed the nucleus of the railway exhibition at Amberley Museum in 1980, the equipment having been little used since 1974. (N.Palmer)

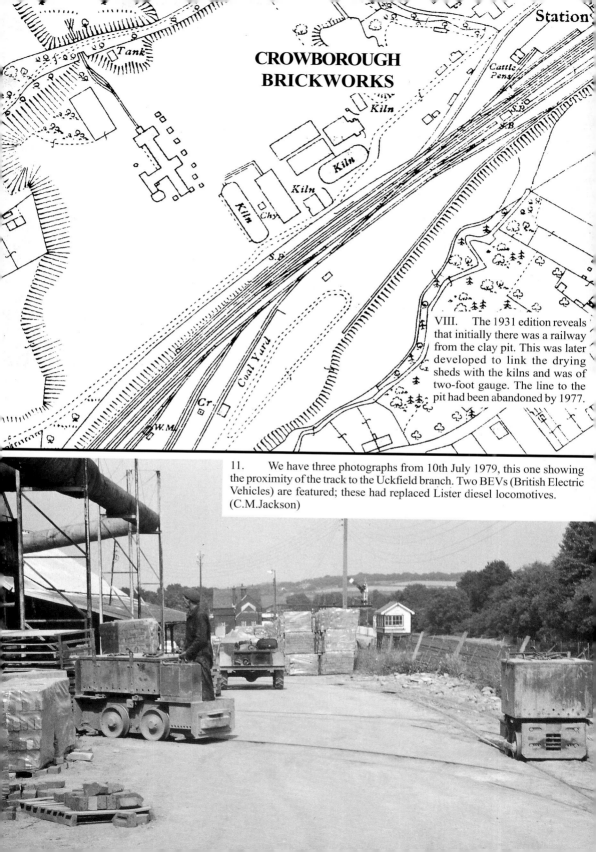

CROWBOROUGH
BRICKWORKS

Station

Tank

Kiln

Kiln

Kiln

Kiln

Chy

S.B.

Cattle Pens

S.B.

S.B.

Coal Yard

Cr.

W.M.

VIII. The 1931 edition reveals that initially there was a railway from the clay pit. This was later developed to link the drying sheds with the kilns and was of two-foot gauge. The line to the pit had been abandoned by 1977.

11. We have three photographs from 10th July 1979, this one showing the proximity of the track to the Uckfield branch. Two BEVs (British Electric Vehicles) are featured; these had replaced Lister diesel locomotives. (C.M.Jackson)

12.   Trays of green bricks are being hauled from the moulding shed to the drying area. On the left is the main line and the former goods shed, which is beyond the lower border of the map. The premises had been acquired by Redland Brick in 1961. (C.M.Jackson)

13.   We survey the kilns as the driver looks at his controller. There were three continuous kilns. The works closed in 1980, having been in use for about 100 years. Its bricks had been used in the reconstruction of Victoria station. (C.M.Jackson)

EAST SUSSEX TRANSPORT
AND TRADING COMPANY -
CUCKMERE HAVEN

14.   A later style Motor Rail diesel stands near the northern terminus as a Southdown bus proceeds from Eastbourne to Seaford. The line closed in 1964, having been established in the early 1930s. (G.E.Baddeley)

IX.   This firm extracted gravel from the beach at Cuckmere Haven and conveyed it on a one-mile long two-foot gauge line to Exceat. It is shown on this 1938 edition of the 6ins to 1 mile survey.

GYPSUM MINES LTD - MOUNTFIELD

15.   The Sub-Wealden Gypsum Company sunk a vertical shaft in 1876 and another followed later, both having colliery-type headgear. The works was set in dense woodland west of the Tonbridge to Hastings main line from which a mile long branch was built. To improve efficiency, an inclined adit was dug in 1945 and fitted with two-foot gauge tracks. Its approach is on the right. (Authors coll.)

16.   Loaded wagons are seen ascending on 11th August 1951. There were two battery electric locomotives on site, but they were little used. The rock was crushed and used for the production of plaster, plasterboard and in cement manufacture, notably at Northfleet. (J.H.Meredith)

HALL & CO. - THE CRUMBLES

17.　　The Crumbles is a massive deposit of marine shingle east of Eastbourne, on a scale approaching that at Dungeness. It had been removed in standard gauge wagons for many decades, evidence of a recently lifted siding being included in this 1950 westward view towards Walllis Avenue, which was then on the edge of Eastbourne. It is on the left of the map. (S.C.Nash)

18.　　The following three close-ups date from 31st March 1964. This is LO2, a Motor Rail with the works number of 5646 and with weather protection of questionable performance. (C.G.Down)

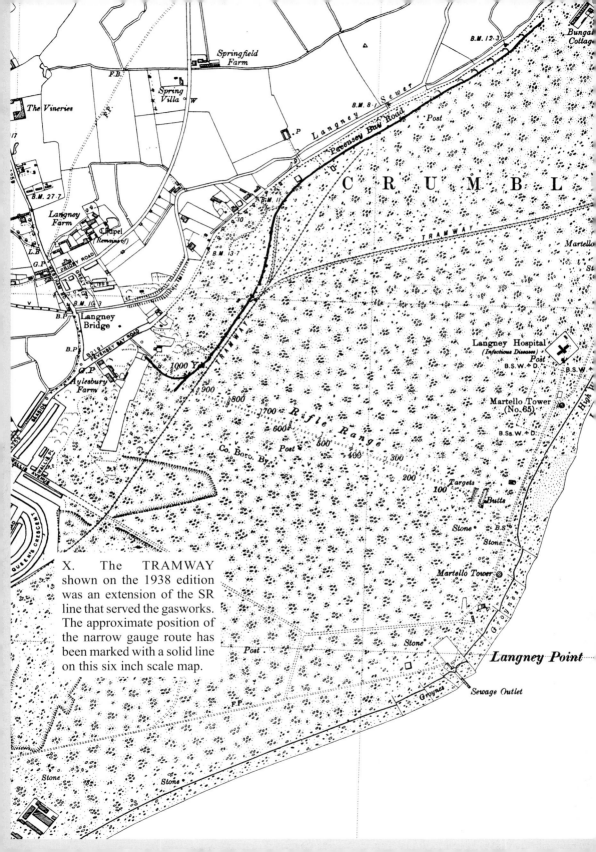

X. The TRAMWAY shown on the 1938 edition was an extension of the SR line that served the gasworks. The approximate position of the narrow gauge route has been marked with a solid line on this six inch scale map.

19. Another of Hall's locomotives that worked out on The Crumbles was Hibberd no. 2163. It stands out of use near the repair shop. (C.G.Down)

20. Numbered in the fleet LO19 was Hunslet no. 3589 of 1947. It is on the right, partly dismantled, while behind are Hibberds numbered 2187 and 2188. The end was nigh. (C.G.Down)

HEAVERS - CHICHESTER

21.　　The firm had four Listers and four Rustons over the years. After closure, some of the wagons were renovated by members of the Hants & Sussex Area Group of the Festiniog Railway Society for use on the Deviation of the line in Wales. (M.J.Sheppard)

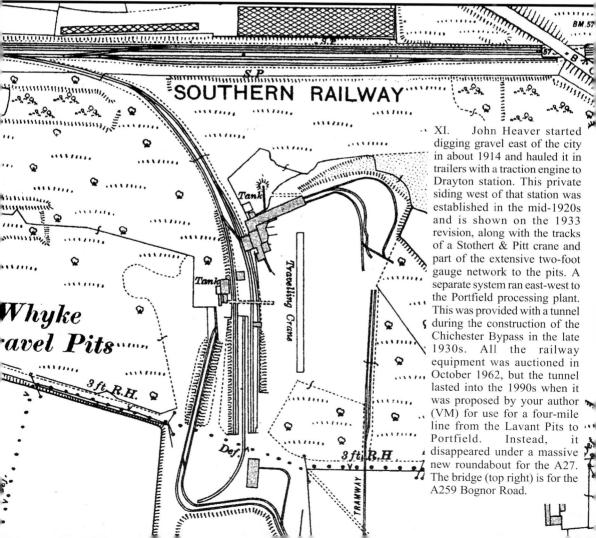

XI.　　John Heaver started digging gravel east of the city in about 1914 and hauled it in trailers with a traction engine to Drayton station. This private siding west of that station was established in the mid-1920s and is shown on the 1933 revision, along with the tracks of a Stothert & Pitt crane and part of the extensive two-foot gauge network to the pits. A separate system ran east-west to the Portfield processing plant. This was provided with a tunnel during the construction of the Chichester Bypass in the late 1930s. All the railway equipment was auctioned in October 1962, but the tunnel lasted into the 1990s when it was proposed by your author (VM) for use for a four-mile line from the Lavant Pits to Portfield. Instead, it disappeared under a massive new roundabout for the A27. The bridge (top right) is for the A259 Bognor Road.

LUDLAY BRICK & TILE CO - BERWICK

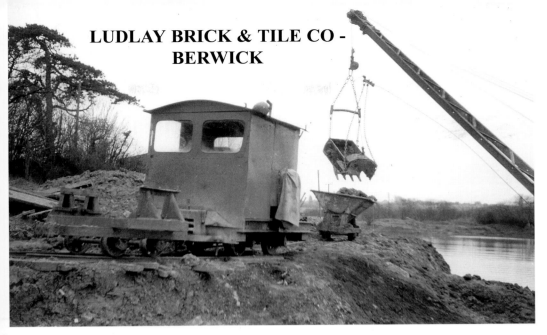

22.   The works was established by 1880 and was situated close to Berwick Church. Photographed in March 1964 is a Trojan engined locomotive, a sheet covering the characteristic radiator of the Croydon-built van. The nearest wagon comprises two Hudson frames, which resulted in an end-tipper. Those seen in picture 21 were also combined in this manner. (C.G.Down)

23.   Two photographs from August 1968 show the end of the pit line and the bottom of the incline. Bricks had only been produced seasonally until about 1950. (C.G.Down)

24.	The works closed in 1965 and remained derelict for over 20 years. The abandoned locomotive is showing its bulging radiator, which is seen better in picture no. 8 in *Industrial Railways of the South-East*. (C.G.Down)

MIDHURST WHITES

25.   Lord Cowdray owned most of the land in the Midhurst area and amongst his family firms was S.Pearson & Son, international civil engineers. A plan was made to construct a tunnel to the Isle of Wight and to line it with sand/lime bricks to be made at a new works on his land, nearly one mile southwest of Midhurst. The plant was built in 1913 and other uses were found for the bricks. The lime was brought by road from Cocking and vast quantities of sand were dug west of the works. This necessitated three separate 2ft 6ins gauge lines at one period, this one being photographed in December 1955. The BR branch line from Petersfield had closed earlier that year, which may account for the use of standard gauge sleepers. The pit was soon extended across its trackbed. (E.Wilmshurst)

26.   "R.Hudson Ltd. Leeds" is evident in the main casting of this "Go-Go Tractor", which was recorded abandoned in June 1969. In the background are the white bricks, which soon became grey. However, they were a good engineering brick owing to their high compressive strength. No. 45913 was fitted with a Fordson engine and is an exhibit at Amberley Museum. (C.M.Jackson)

27.   A Simplex was found abandoned in its shed on the upper line on 11th April 1980. Owing to poor compression, the photographer was able to wind the starting handle on the right to move it out. Three points were not removed by the scrapmen and could still be seen in 2001. (C.M.Jackson)

28.   This photograph was taken on the same day, not long before the demolition of the works. Parts of two brick presses stand on small wagons, which had previously carried new bricks via the traverser in the foreground into massive horizontal autoclaves (steam pressurised cylinders with doors at one end). Herein they were cured, while on the wagons, for up to 12 hours and then many were subsequently loaded into wagons on the siding provided by the LSWR. It had been in the centre of this eastward view. On the right is a battered Simplex. (C.M.Jackson)

PENFOLDS LTD - EARTHAM

29.   Penfolds had a builders merchant business and extracted gravel from the coastal plain about five miles east of Chichester, close to the A27. Two pictures record their locomotives on 4th August 1963, shortly after the line had closed. This is a gutted Ruston. (C.G.Down)

30.   More unusual was a type MD2 Orenstein & Koppel, numbered 7176. The track passed under a lane in a concrete tube. (C.G.Down)

PETT LEVEL TRAMWAY

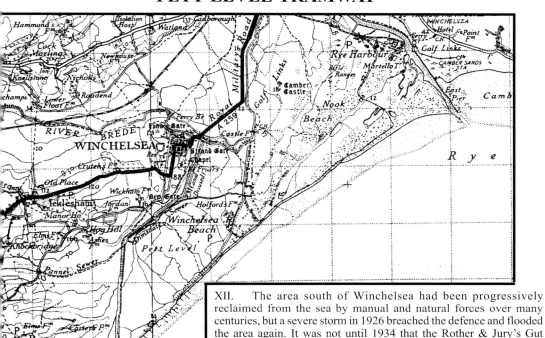

XII.   The area south of Winchelsea had been progressively reclaimed from the sea by manual and natural forces over many centuries, but a severe storm in 1926 breached the defence and flooded the area again. It was not until 1934 that the Rother & Jury's Gut Catchment Board (gut = outflow) could find funds for new defences to be built. Work started at Cliff End (lower left), where there was road access to a new two-foot gauge railway. This was built along the foreshore to link up with track of Simpson (Rye Harbour) Ltd, 220yds inland and near one of their gravel pits. Part is missing on this 1940 edition at 1ins to 1 mile owing to anti-invasion measures, which also included flooding Pett Level. After reclamation work in 1946, the tramway was largely abandoned.

1.   A postcard view shows the completed embankment, which carried the tramway. The line had almost reached Winchelsea Lifeboat Station by 1936. The eastern link was made in 1937, giving a complete run of about five miles. (Hastings Library)

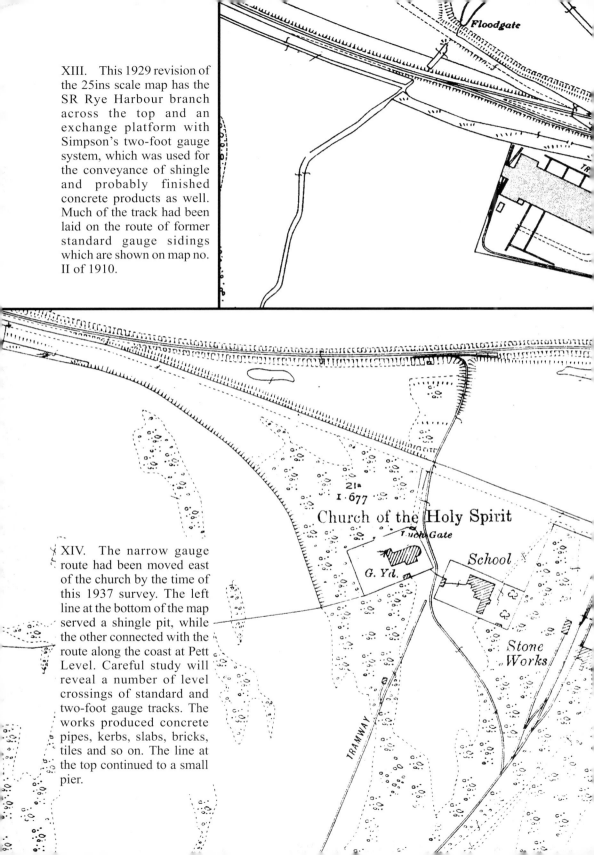

Floodgate

XIII.   This 1929 revision of the 25ins scale map has the SR Rye Harbour branch across the top and an exchange platform with Simpson's two-foot gauge system, which was used for the conveyance of shingle and probably finished concrete products as well. Much of the track had been laid on the route of former standard gauge sidings which are shown on map no. II of 1910.

21ᵃ
I·677

Church of the Holy Spirit
Lych Gate

G. Yd.

School

XIV.   The narrow gauge route had been moved east of the church by the time of this 1937 survey. The left line at the bottom of the map served a shingle pit, while the other connected with the route along the coast at Pett Level. Careful study will reveal a number of level crossings of standard and two-foot gauge tracks. The works produced concrete pipes, kerbs, slabs, bricks, tiles and so on. The line at the top continued to a small pier.

Stone Works

TRAMWAY

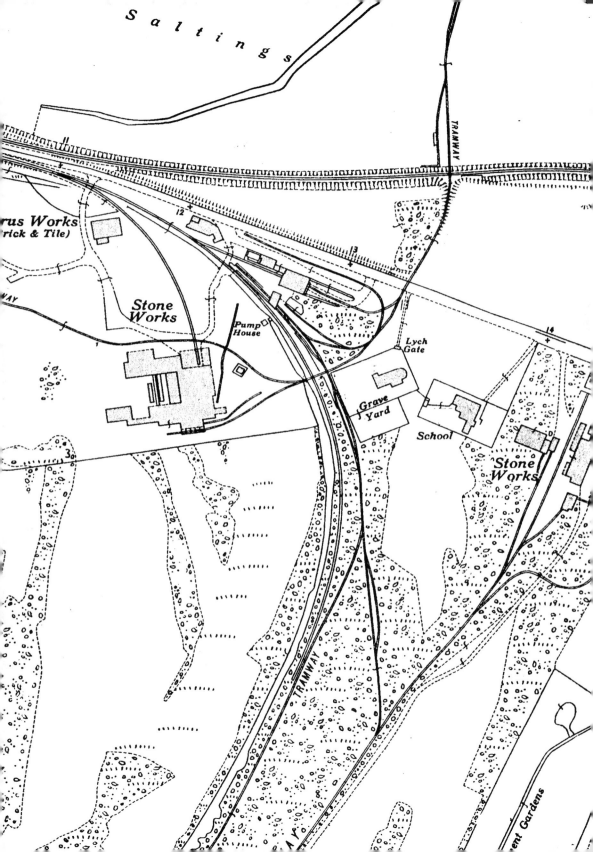

S a l t i n g s

TRAMWAY

rus Works
(rick & Tile)

12

3

Stone
Works

Pump
House

Lych
Gate

Grave
Yard

School

Stone
Works

14

3

TRAMWAY

ent Gardens

32. It seems that a fairly heavy rail was employed, but no records can be traced. Lightweight "Jubilee" track was employed on the temporary branches and many timber bolster wagons were provided. (Hastings Library)

33. The RJGCB purchased Simplex no. 7025 in 1935 and another followed soon after. There was also the usual fleet of skip wagons. Much of the track was repaired in 1946, but only a short unused section at the west end could be seen by 1953. (Hastings Library)

THAKEHAM TILES - STORRINGTON

XV.   The 1937 revision of the 25ins to 1 mile map shows the extent of the works which, by that time, had been in operation for at least three years. It was situated one mile north-east of Storrington on Heath Common.

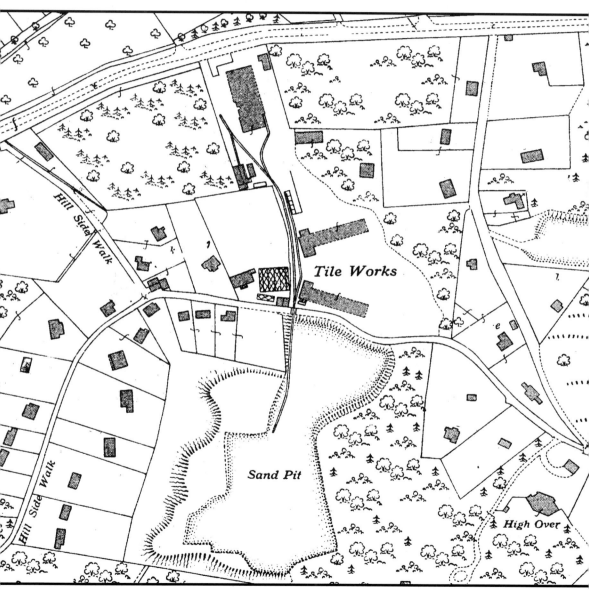

34.   Three photographs from the Summer of 1979 show Hudson-Hunslet no. 3653 at work. It was built in 1948 and is seen here at the loading hopper. (C.M.Jackson)

35.   Black exhaust is being discharged as the engine passes between stacks of tiles and the loco shed. The firm used home made locomotives until the 1960s, after which period it purchased diesels second hand. This one had previously worked at Enfield Rolling Mills. (C.M.Jackson)

36.   This is the tipping shed at the end of the journey where the track passes over a footpath. The last train ran on 14th November 1980 and the entire system was donated to Amberley Museum. This included two locomotives; another came from Ibstock Brick Laybrook, two miles to the north. At the time these photos were taken the line ran only about 100yds from a sand-hopper to the works. (C.M.Jackson)

WARNHAM
BRICKWORKS

37.   The railway in the pit was 2ft 6ins gauge and Simplex diesel locomotives were used to shunt wagons near the working face. All three pictures were taken on 22nd December 1964. (A.Neale)

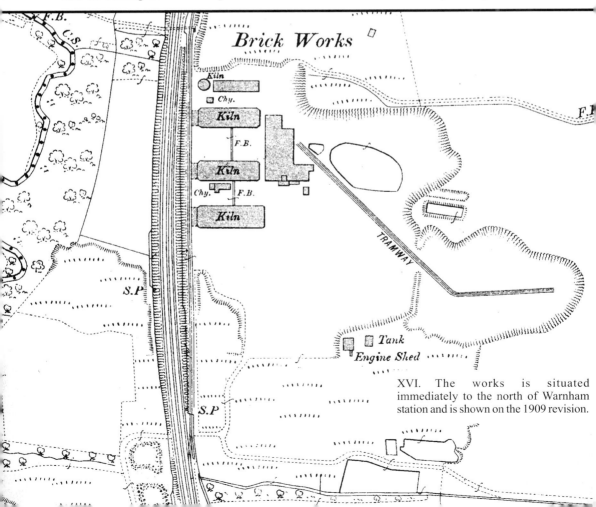

XVI. The works is situated immediately to the north of Warnham station and is shown on the 1909 revision.

38.   On the main part of their journey, the wagons were attached to an endless moving cable and a stay prevented runaways on the uphill section. It is lowered on the old two-plank wagon and raised onto a bracket on the newer three-plank type. One wagon was saved after closure in 1965 and is at the Amberley Museum. (A.Neale)

39.   There are rollers between the rails to support the steel rope and the uphill track has a continuous ratchet alongside to receive the stay or pawl. There was a 2ft gauge line at the upper level. This was locomotive worked and lasted until about 1971. (A.Neale)

2. Pleasure
AMBERLEY WORKING MUSEUM

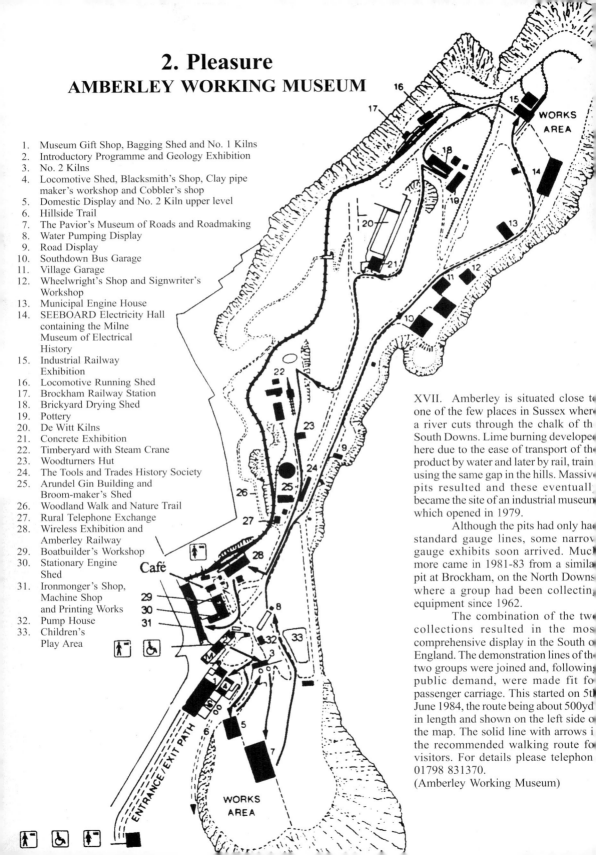

1. Museum Gift Shop, Bagging Shed and No. 1 Kilns
2. Introductory Programme and Geology Exhibition
3. No. 2 Kilns
4. Locomotive Shed, Blacksmith's Shop, Clay pipe maker's workshop and Cobbler's shop
5. Domestic Display and No. 2 Kiln upper level
6. Hillside Trail
7. The Pavior's Museum of Roads and Roadmaking
8. Water Pumping Display
9. Road Display
10. Southdown Bus Garage
11. Village Garage
12. Wheelwright's Shop and Signwriter's Workshop
13. Municipal Engine House
14. SEEBOARD Electricity Hall containing the Milne Museum of Electrical History
15. Industrial Railway Exhibition
16. Locomotive Running Shed
17. Brockham Railway Station
18. Brickyard Drying Shed
19. Pottery
20. De Witt Kilns
21. Concrete Exhibition
22. Timberyard with Steam Crane
23. Woodturners Hut
24. The Tools and Trades History Society
25. Arundel Gin Building and Broom-maker's Shed
26. Woodland Walk and Nature Trail
27. Rural Telephone Exchange
28. Wireless Exhibition and Amberley Railway
29. Boatbuilder's Workshop
30. Stationary Engine Shed
31. Ironmonger's Shop, Machine Shop and Printing Works
32. Pump House
33. Children's Play Area

XVII. Amberley is situated close to one of the few places in Sussex where a river cuts through the chalk of the South Downs. Lime burning developed here due to the ease of transport of the product by water and later by rail, train using the same gap in the hills. Massive pits resulted and these eventually became the site of an industrial museum which opened in 1979.

Although the pits had only had standard gauge lines, some narrow gauge exhibits soon arrived. Much more came in 1981-83 from a similar pit at Brockham, on the North Downs where a group had been collecting equipment since 1962.

The combination of the two collections resulted in the most comprehensive display in the South of England. The demonstration lines of the two groups were joined and, following public demand, were made fit for passenger carriage. This started on 5th June 1984, the route being about 500yds in length and shown on the left side of the map. The solid line with arrows is the recommended walking route for visitors. For details please telephone 01798 831370.
(Amberley Working Museum)

40.   Among the exhibits from Brockham in the early years were two 3ft 2¼ins gauge 0-4-0Ts built by Fletcher Jennings in 1880. They had worked at the nearby Betchworth Quarry, which is shown in pictures 86-93 in our *Guildford to Redhill* album, and were named *Townsend Hook* and *William Finlay*. (F.Hornby)

41.   Another photograph from August 1986 shows that some covered accommodation had been created by that time, the supports being former telephone poles. The Ruston is no. 187081 from 1937 and the Hudson Hunslet is *Blue Star*. (F.Hornby)

42.   A station was created behind the Wireless Hall and is the nearest one to the entrance. Passengers are conveyed usually in vehicles built for the transport of workers, this example being from RAF Fauld, in Staffordshire. The locomotive is *Blue Star*. (F.Hornby)

43.   The route between the stations resembles a nature trail, evidence of chalk quarrying having been obliterated. A demonstration train of skips is hauled by *Redland*, an Orenstein & Koppel product in 1937. (P.G.Barnes)

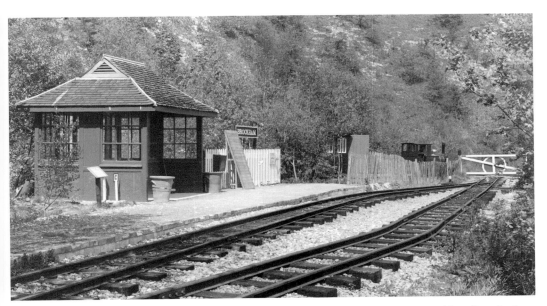

44.   A loop was also provided at the upper terminus, which was named "Brockham" and where an ex-Brighton Corporation Tramway's waiting shelter was erected. In the background is *Polar Bear* and its shed. (V.Mitchell)

45.   Two-foot gauge no. 18 *Lion* was built in the USA by Baldwin in 1917 for use in World War I. The 4-6-0T spent most of its working life in India and was sent to the Leighton Buzzard Railway for major repairs, after being a static exhibit here for several years. (V.Mitchell)

46.　　No. 27 was built by Motor Rail Ltd in 1934 to the Simplex design which had been produced prior to World War I. It was used by Joseph Arnold at Leighton Buzzard. (F.Hornby)

────────────▶

47.　　Some photographs from 1987 feature other exhibits. Built by Orenstein & Koppel in 1907, no. 740 was imported from India, where it had worked on the Matheran Railway. It was one of four supplied to that line and is illustrated in *Two-foot Gauge Survivors* (Middleton Press). It was a temporary exhibit here. (P.Groom)

────────────▶

48.　　The simplest form of industrial locomotive has dumb buffers, one brake block each side, a transverse seat, no cab sides and an unusually low number. It is an Orenstein & Koppel from 1936 and was rebuilt to 3ft 2¼ins gauge in 1945 for use at the Betchworth Western Whitestone Pit. It is named *Monty*, a corruption of the UK supplier's trade name. (P.Groom)

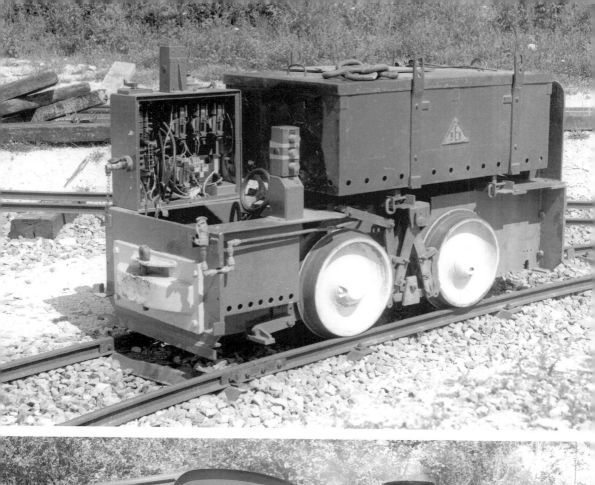

49.   Another simple machine on show was the BEV - British Electric Vehicles. Commonly used in mines, the battery box could be hoisted off and easily replaced. It was made by Wingrove and Rogers in 1953 and was one of three on site. This example came from North Holmwood Brickworks. (P.Groom)

50.   French manufacturers were represented by this 1947 Decauville (no. 1126), which was photographed after completion of restoration in 1987, but before final painting and refitting of side tanks. It carries the name *Barbouilleur.* (P.Groom)

51.   No. 3101 is a rare example of a Simplex to be shown with full armour. Built at the end of World War I, it has screw threaded rods supporting the roof, allowing its height to be adjusted according to the intensity of surrounding gunfire. (P.G.Barnes)

52.   Visiting the 1987 Railway Gala was the 1921 Baguley *Rishra*. The tunnel had given access to another chalk pit and was used subsequently for the storage of exhibits. The nameboard MAIN STRIKE MINE was applied during the making of a James Bond film in 1984. (P.G.Barnes)

53.   One of the most unusual exhibits was capable of operating on 1ft 10ins and 5ft 3ins gauges. Built in Dublin in 1920 by William Spence and Son for the Guinness Brewery, this small engine could work in a "haulage truck" on the wider tracks. It would be lifted therein using the hoist seen on the right of picture no. 45. It was photographed in the 1986 Exhibition Hall in 1994. (M.Turvey)

54.   We now have four views from 1995. *Polar Bear* and its coaches had operated at Groudle Glen, a pleasure park and small zoo on the east coast of the Isle of Man. Manufactured in 1905, the 2-4-0T was unusual in having a marine boiler, which helped to achieve the engine's elegant proportions. (M.Turvey)

55.   Shunting operations were recorded near the bottom points of the top loop. *The Major* was of German origin, having been constructed by Orenstein & Koppel in 1937. It was used by the Dorking Greystone & Lime Company at Betchworth. (M.Turvey)

56.   Built by Ransomes & Rapier in 1937, the nearest locomotive is attached to a Post Office Railway mailbag carrier. No. 808 dates from 1930 and was one of many driverless trains electrically operated in small tube tunnels under London. The new platform on the right was for use at busy times. (M.Turvey)

57.   *Scaldwell* stands on 3ft gauge track and is a long-term static exhibit. It was completed by Peckett in 1913 and hauled ironstone in Northamptonshire for most of its life. (M.Turvey)

58.   Coasting downhill on 30th June 1996 is *Peter*, a Bagnall 0-4-0ST from 1918. It is approaching the loop points and is on the points to the wood yard siding. The single line staff has just been surrendered and it will be used to unlock the seven-lever ground frame. (M.Turvey)

59.   With the main line on the left, *Peldon* proceeds towards the wood yard on 13th September 1998. This four-wheeled diesel was built by John Fowler in 1936 in Leeds. The maximum gradient on the passenger route is 1 in 43. (P.G.Barnes)

60.   *Peldon* stands in the saw mill during an annual event billed as "Wood from the Trees". The museum has many special days devoted to specific trades and forms of transport. (P.G.Barnes)

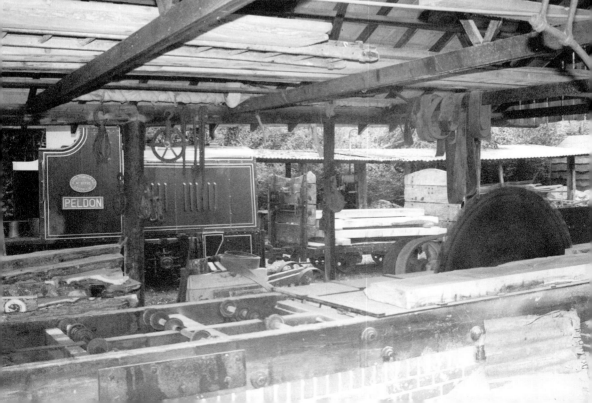

61.   We can now enjoy six photos from the 2000 Railway Gala weekend, when *Cloister* was the visiting locomotive. The 0-4-0ST Hunslet of 1891 was normally resident at the Kew Bridge Steam Museum. The hose on the track was for charging train emergency air brakes from a lineside compressor, each locomotive having an air valve for applications. (P.G.Barnes)

62.   The steam line-up comprised the diminutive *Polar Bear*, the completed *Barbouilleur* and the ex-Penrhyn Quarry *Cloister*. In the background is the workshop, and on the right is the Exhibition Hall, which contains relics from narrow gauge industrial lines throughout Great Britain. (P.G.Barnes)

63.   Betchworth Hall was erected during 1996-99 using materials from a saw mill at Handcross. It was built around the shed glimpsed in picture no. 44; this structure was soon dismantled. Note the extra platform and that rainwater is collected for pumping to the locomotives via the hose above the fence. (P.G.Barnes)

64.   Betchworth Hall gave long-awaited additional accommodation and was provided with both 2ft and 3ft 2¼ins gauge tracks, but no smoke vents as it was intended for clean engines. *Peldon* is on the left. Enough components were left over to build a steam locomotive shed. (P.G.Barnes)

65.   This view has Brockham station and the new hall in the background and some dual gauge track on the right. The line on the left curves into the locomotive storage area and in the middle distance are three BEVs coupled to a rail wagon. (P.G.Barnes)

66.   Looking in the other direction from near the BEVs, we see a display of temporary way on the left. As the museum entered the new century, plans were made for the line in the centre to be upgraded so that passengers could be carried around the head of the quarry as far as the Electricity Hall. (P.G.Barnes)

DEVIL'S DYKE
STEEP GRADE RAILWAY

67.   This funicular line was built to the gauge of three feet on the scarp edge of the South Downs, five miles northwest of Brighton. It was intended to entertain visitors from that town who might wish to descend to Poynings at 3mph. It opened on 24th July 1897, but the lower station was never built. (R.J.Harley coll.)

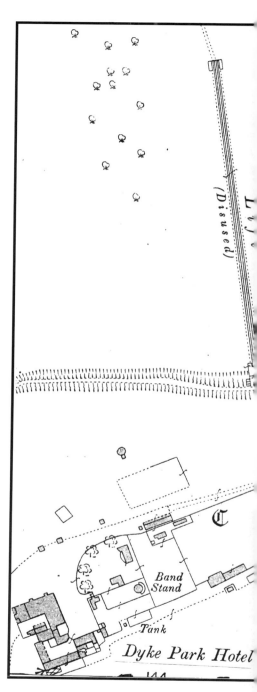

XVIII. The 1909 revision shows the relationship of the line to the only other public building in the area.

68.   Poynings had little to offer trippers, except afternoon tea in a few cottages. The winding house contained a Hornsby-Ackroyd oil engine to wind the 60-strand steel cable on a five-foot diameter pulley. (P.Hay coll.)

69.   The two tanks outside the station contained cooling water for the 25hp engine. The gradient ranged from 1 in 2.9 to 1 in 1.5, but the cars were designed with a 30° inclination. Financial problems and dwindling traffic brought closure in 1908. (P.Hay coll.)

70.   Each car seated 12 people and had gripper brakes on the rails. Brake wheels are shown on both platforms. The line rose 395ft on its 840ft length. (The Engineer)

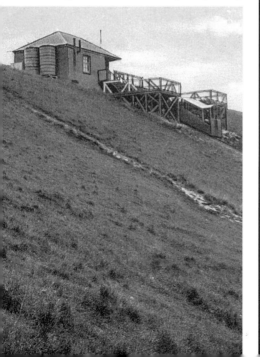

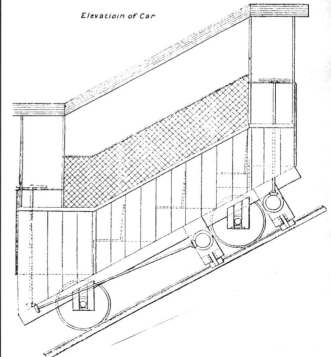

Elevation of Car

DRUSILLAS PARK - ALFRISTON

71.   The founder was Captain Douglas Ann who purchased the site in 1923 and laid down an endless 9½ins gauge track in 1935. The first locomotive was *Ranmore*, a model D class LBSCR 0-4-2T, and the second was a freelance affair built around a Citroen 7 petrol engine. The track was moved after World War II began and used for target practice by Canadians prior to the Dieppe Raid in 1942. (C.J.Huggett)

72.   A new two-foot gauge circuit was laid in 1946 and a "Planet" with 10hp Ford engine purchased from Hibberds. It ran until 1974 and went to Dover Transport Museum in 1988. It was replaced by a 1943 Ruston, which was given this steam outline at Hove Engineerium and named *Emily*. (Drusillas Park)

73.   An additional locomotive was required and this came in 1978 in the form of a 1948 Simplex. The original petrol engine was replaced by a Perkins diesel and it was named *Bill*. A 1965 Simplex was purchased in 1988 and steam outline panels made for it. For details of operating days, please telephone 01323 874100. (D.Trevor Rowe)

EASTBOURNE TRAMWAY

74.   Claude W. Lane built electric delivery vehicles in Barnet and constructed a 15ins gauge miniature tram in 1949. A short track was laid down on the seafront at St. Leonards for the 1951 Summer season only. Car 3 was built for his short-lived line in Rhyl and is seen in the Eastbourne works in 1962, long after it had been regauged. (T.Wright)

XIX.   The Eastbourne track was laid on The Crumbles to the gauge of two feet, work starting at the east end in March 1954. The section from Royal Parade to Golf House opened in stages in 1954 to early 1955, the part to the Car Depot in July 1955 and to the curve beyond in 1956, the line being completed in 1958.

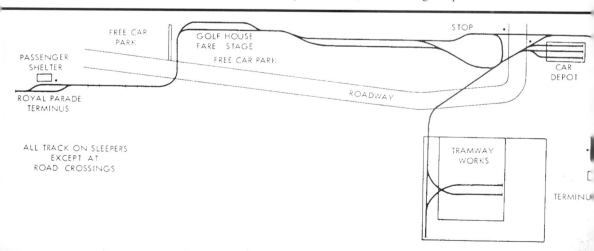

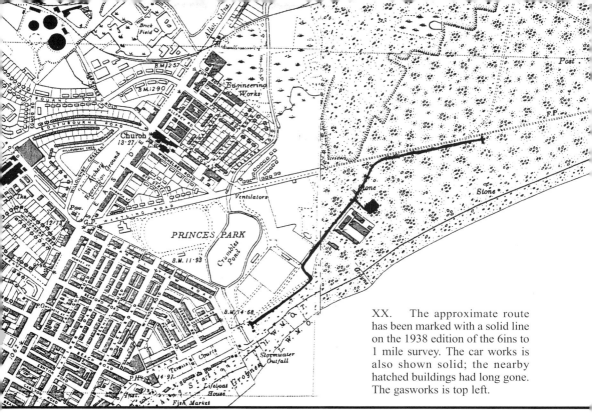

XX.   The approximate route has been marked with a solid line on the 1938 edition of the 6ins to 1 mile survey. The car works is also shown solid; the nearby hatched buildings had long gone. The gasworks is top left.

75.   The Royal Parade terminus is seen in July 1962. Later, a siding was provided for a tram shop and an unloading area was created this side of the loop. Car 7 was built at Eastbourne in 1958 in the style of a Llandudno & Colwyn Bay tram. (T.Wright)

76.   Car 7 is approaching Golf House on its way to The Crumbles in September 1969. The top deck was always popular; the new cars had full size controllers and brake handles. (S.C.Nash)

77.   Car 6 is on its way from The Crumbles on 22nd June 1960 and is crossing Wartling Road. Its main difference from no. 7 is ease of access to the end seats on the lower deck. (S.C.Nash)

78.   Outside the Car Works in July 1962 is car 6, the upper seats of which came from a Bournemouth tram that had been transferred to work on the Llandudno & Colwyn Bay system. (T.Wright)

Other views can be found in
Seaton and Eastbourne Tramways
(Middleton Press).

79.   Leaving Royal Parade for The Crumbles in July 1962 is car 4, a replica of Blackpool Tramway's "Boat" design. Finished in green and cream both the original and its copy are still popular on fine days, the latter in its new location - see caption 81. (T.Wright)

80.   Returning across the shingle from The Crumbles in June 1960 is car 238, which was constructed in 1955, as a replica of another much loved Blackpool design. It could not cope with crowds quickly and was sold to an American. (S.C.Nash)

81.   Car 7 is seen again, this time in July 1962 at the end of the line (lower left) at The Crumbles. Sadly a dispute arose with Eastbourne Corporation and the tramway closed on 17th September 1969. It was regauged to 2ft 9ins and moved to Seaton in Devon where it can still be enjoyed. (T.Wright)

GREAT BUSH RAILWAY - HADLOW DOWN

82.   Traction engine events began in Tinkers Park in the mid-1960s and a short 8½ins gauge steam operated line followed. This was replaced by a two-foot gauge line in the early 1970s and this Motor Rail became the first locomotive. Named *Aminal*, it has been seen earlier in pictures 22-24 and was photographed on 31st May 1975. (D.Trevor Rowe)

83.   No. 5 *Alpha* was recorded in May 1989 during track extension work. It is a 1937 Ruston & Hornsby and has been seen already in picture no. 2 at Rodmell. (I.Oughton)

84.   In the background is BEV no. 22 *Lama* of 1953 and nearer to us is BEV no. 24 *Titch* of 1972. They are part of the fleet shown at Crowborough in pictures 11 to 13. (I.Oughton)

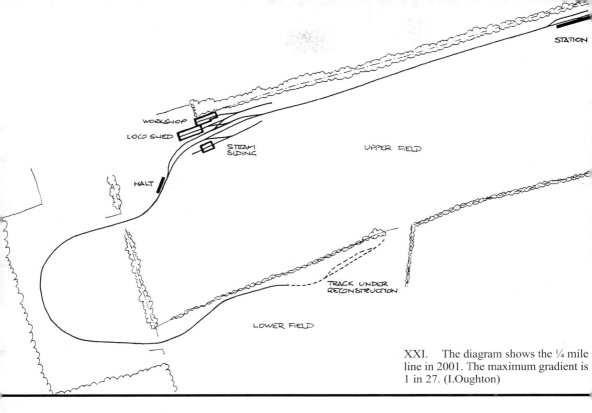

WORKSHOP
LOCO SHED
STEAM SIDING
HALT
UPPER FIELD
TRACK UNDER RECONSTRUCTION
LOWER FIELD
STATION

XXI.   The diagram shows the ¼ mile line in 2001. The maximum gradient is 1 in 27. (I.Oughton)

85.   *Albany* had been built in 1941 for the Woolwich Arsenal 18ins gauge system by Ruston & Hornsby and it remained there until 1971. It was on the Isle of Wight from 1973 and it underwent gauge conversion there. (I.Oughton)

86.   A view from September 1990 reveals the little known complex trackwork. Centre stage is no. 14 *Albany*. (I.Oughton)

87. We now have two photographs from 6th June 1999 - the railway is only open for the weekend following the Whitsun Bank Holiday. In steam was no. 2 *Sezela No. 2* which, along with no. 6, spent its working life hauling sugar cane in the Natal province of South Africa with a variety of 20 others. (I.Oughton)

Locomotive list

No	Name	Form	Class	Maker	No	Date	Notes	
1	AMINAL	4wPM	20/35hp	Motor Rail	?	c 1931	(a)	(1)
2	SEZELA No 2	0-4-0T OC		Avonside	1720	1915	(b)	(2)
3	GOAT	4wDM	R	Lister	8022	1936	(c)	(3)
4	MILD	4wDM	20/28hp	Motor Rail	8687	1941	(c)	(2)
5	ALPHA	4wDM	44/48hp	Ruston	183744	1937	(d)	(2)
6	SEZELA No 6	0-4-0T OC		Avonside	1928	1923	(e)	(1)
7	FIDO	4wPM	20/35hp	Motor Rail	5297	1931	(f)	(4)
8	TUESDAY	4wDM		Hibberd	2586	c 1941	(f)	(5)
9	SMIFSAGIT	4wDM		Hudson	3109	1944	(f)	(6)
10	CAPE	4wDM	RL1a	O&K	5926	1935	(g)	(7)
11	LAYER	4wDM	Resilient	Fowler	21294	1936	(h)	(8)
12	-	4wDM		Hibberd	2163	1938	(j)	(9)
	PETER PAN	0-4-0ST OC	Wren	Kerr Stuart	4256	1922	(k)	
14	ALBANY	4wDM	20DL	Ruston	213840	1941	(l)	(2)
15	OLDE	4wDM		Hudson	2176	1940	(m)	(10)
16	Number not allocated							
17	BEAR	4wDM	30DL	Ruston	339209	1952	(n)	(8)
18	OWL	4wDM	30DL	Ruston	283513	1949	(p)	(8)
19	-	4wDM		Hibberd	2631	c 1942	(q)	(11)
20	-	0-4-0BE		W&R	4634	1951	(r)	(12)
21	-	4wBE		W&R	5035	1954	(r)	(12)
22	LAMA	4wBE		W&R	5033	1953	(s)	(2)
23	-	0-4-0BE	W417	W&R	M7534	1972	(t)	(12)
24	TITCH	0-4-0BE	W417	W&R	M7535	1972	(t)	(2)
25	WOLF	4wDM	20/28hp	Motor Rail	7469	1940	(u)	(2)
26	No. 4	4wDM	12hp	Ruston	177638	1936	(v)	(2)
27	TWENTYTWO	4wDM	20DL	Ruston	226302	1944	(v)	(2)
28	TWENTYFOUR	4wDM	30DL	Ruston	382820	1955	(w)	(2)

88.   Visiting for the weekend was *Jack*, built by Andrew Barclay as no. 1871 in 1925 for Granton Gasworks. *Albany* is on the right and in the shed is *Peter Pan*, a "Wren" class 0-4-0ST from Kerr Stuart in 1922, normally resident on the Leighton Buzzard Railway. (I.Oughton)

Notes on locomotives

(a)	ex Ludlay Brick & Tile, Berwick, East Sussex. 1969. Received as 4wDM
(b)	ex J. Hurst & Sons, Andover, Hampshire. 1 May 1977
(c)	ex Redland Bricks, Crowborough Brickworks, East Sussex. 1972
(d)	ex Alpha Cement Co., Rodmell, East Sussex. November 1975
(e)	ex J. Hurst & Sons, Andover, Hampshire. 7 July 1976
(f)	ex Island Narrow Gauge Group, Albany, Isle of Wight. 15 August 1976
(g)	ex Cape Universal Products Ltd, Uxbridge, Middlesex. 4 December 1976. 2' 6" gauge
(h)	ex Brockham Museum, Surrey. March 1977
(j)	ex Horam Brick Co., Horam Brickworks, East Sussex. 1973
(k)	temporary storage Sept 1977 to May 1978
(l)	ex Island Narrow Gauge Group, Albany, Isle of Wight. 3 November 1977
(m)	ex Brockham Museum, Surrey. 3 November 1977
(n)	ex Alan Keef, Cote, Oxfordshire. 16 September 1978
(p)	ex Mill Lane Commercials, Sandiacre, Derbyshire. 29 August 1978
(q)	ex Bredgar and Wormshill Light Railway, Sittingbourne, Kent. 19 May 1979
(r)	ex Redland Bricks, Crowborough Brickworks, East Sussex. 19 March 1980
(s)	ex Redland Bricks, Crowborough Brickworks, East Sussex. 6 May 1980
(t)	ex Redland Bricks, Crowborough Brickworks, East Sussex. April 1981
(u)	ex Bredgar and Wormshill Light Railway, Sittingbourne, Kent. 1990
(v)	ex Surrey Light Railway, Odiham, Hampshire. 28 October 2000
(w)	ex Surrey Light Railway, Odiham, Hampshire. 2001
(1)	Out of use
(2)	Working order
(3)	to Island Narrow Gauge Group, ℅ Surrey Light Railway. 1978
(4)	to Ian Jolly, Mold, Clwyd, North Wales. May 1977
(5)	to Leadhills & Wanlockhead Railway, Lanarkshire, Scotland. 1988
(6)	to Alan Keef, Cote, Oxfordshire. 16 March 1978
(7)	to Amberley Chalk Pits Museum, Hampshire. 11 August 1978
(8)	to Alan Keef, Cote, Oxfordshire. 11 May 1979
(9)	to Cleethorpes Coast Light Railway, Yorkshire. 13 October 1991
(10)	to Bredgar and Wormshill Light Railway, Sittingbourne, Kent. 19 May 1979
(11)	to Leadhills & Wanlockhead Railway, Lanarkshire, Scotland. 13 September 1987
(12)	Used for spares

HOLLYCOMBE
STEAM COLLECTION

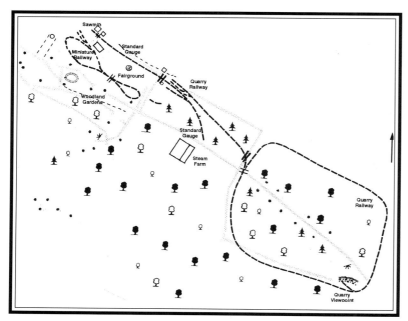

XXII. The extensive wood-land estate 1½ miles south of Liphook was purchased by Commander John Baldock in 1951 and he began to collect items to represent the changes that were taking place in various aspects of transport, agriculture and fairground rides. We look at only the two-foot gauge Quarry Railway, which was started in 1968 and which eventually formed a loop.

89.   No. 38 *Jerry M* was built by Hunslet in 1895 and is seen close to the former Hayling Island platform canopy in June 1985. The 0-4-0ST worked at the Dinorwic Slate Quarries as *Vaenol* and was regauged slightly. In the background (both sides) are standard gauge exhibits. (P.G.Barnes)

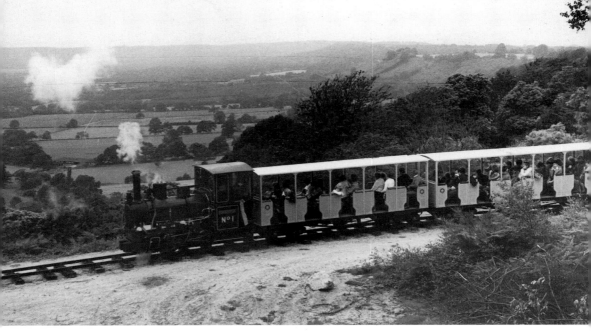

90.   Trains stop at the estate quarry, which is in Lower Greensand, so that visitors can gaze over the western end of the Weald to the South Downs. No. 1 *Caledonia* is against the light in this July 1977 panorama. After completing the loop, trains reverse down the 1 in 37 gradient into the station, the guard using the air brake. The journey length is about 1½ miles. The five coaches came from Ramsgate Tunnel Railway. (D.Trevor Rowe)

91.   A closer look at the same locomotive in April 1988 shows it renumbered 70. It was constructed in 1931 for Durham Water Board by Andrew Barclay Ltd in their Caledonia Works in Kilmarnock and later used at Dinorwic Quarries in Wales. It has a well tank - that is, water between the frames. The line also has *Jack*, a Ruston & Hornsby diesel from RAF Chilmark. The railway has been part of a trust, the Hollycombe Working Steam Museum Ltd, since 1997. For details please telephone 01428 724900.   (T.Heavyside)

RYE & CAMBER TRAMWAY

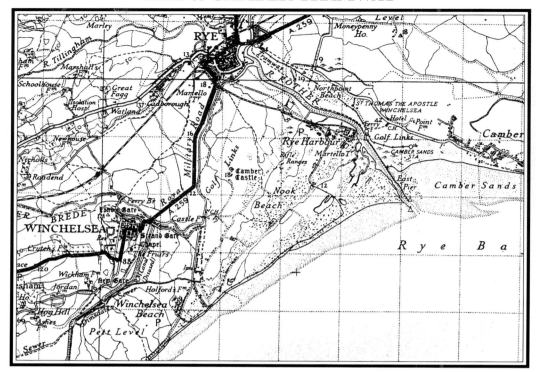

XXIII. The Tramway is shown close to the east bank of the River Rother on the 1940 edition of 1ins to 1 mile Ordnance Survey. It was opened from Rye to Golf Links on 13th July 1895 and extended to Camber Sands on 13th July 1908. Residents of Camber and Rye Harbour used the line until the advent of a bus service in March 1924. The Pett Level line is shown near Winchelsea Beach.

XXIV. The 1854 goods line to Rye Harbour never carried passengers and is illustrated in pictures 38-40 in our *Hastings to Ashford* album. (Railway Magazine)

XXV. The left map is from the 1909 edition and the other was published 20 years later.

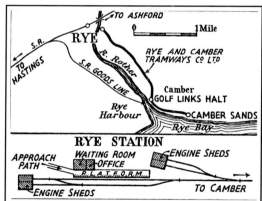

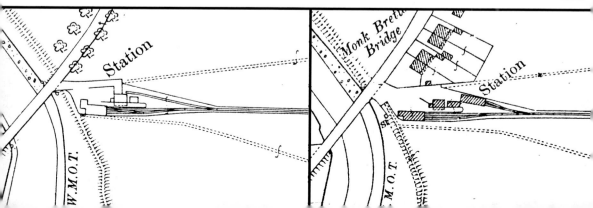

RYE

92.   The earliest known view includes the engine shed before it was doubled in width in 1896, the road bridge over the Rother (left) and the tower of the SECR swing bridge over this river on the right. This was dismantled in 1903. (Colonel Stephens Museum)

93.   *Camber* arrived from Bagnall less than 24 hours before the railway opened. It was only 11ft 3ins long and weighed a mere six tons. On the right is *Victoria* which came from the same builder in 1897 and was so named in honour of the Queen's Diamond Jubilee. It only carrried the name for its first few years and was slightly larger than *Camber*. (R.Shepherd coll.)

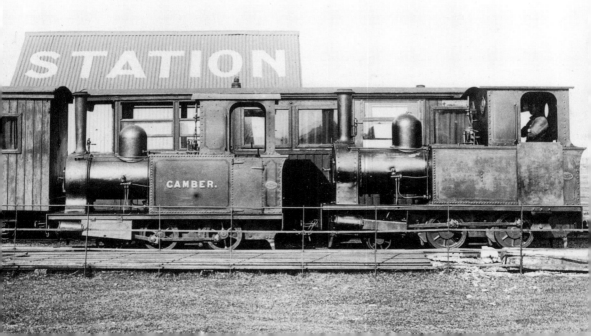

94.　*Camber* lost its lettering in 1921. On the right is the line's first coach, which had been built by Bagnall for the opening. The other was constructed by the Rother Ironworks in Rye and delivered in March 1896. This photo dates from 11th April 1931. (H.C.Casserley)

95.　Seen on the same day is *Camber*, with its locally made cab door. Its original disc driving wheels had been replaced by ones with spokes. Note the shield to protect the slide bars and piston rod from blown sand. (H.C.Casserley)

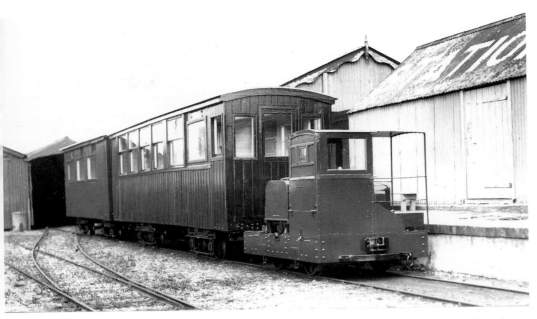

96.   To reduce operating costs, a Simplex style petrol-engined locomotive was purchased new from the Kent Construction Co. Ltd of Ashford in 1924. The photographer was well known for persuading drivers to move locomotives for him and it is likely that this one positioned *Camber* for the two previous pictures. (H.C.Casserley)

97.   The engineer for the construction of the line was H.F.Stephens and he used a standard design of building here and on other railways. Examples survive on the Kent & East Sussex Railway. The roofs had earlier carried the words TRAM STATION TO CAMBER ON SEA, the message being visible from the hilltop town of Rye. (R.S.Carpenter coll.)

98. The shed on the right was added in 1922 and it later usually housed the petrol engine and the two open coaches. It was built on the site of a siding and platform used for sand traffic, which had ceased in about 1916. The water tank is visible behind the engine shed. (R.Shepherd coll.)

99. The cab seen in picture 96 was extended and the small window behind the driver's head was replaced by a droplight. The two-cylinder Dorman engine was exhausted below the front buffer via the curved tube. This and the next photo date from 29th July 1939. (S.W.Baker)

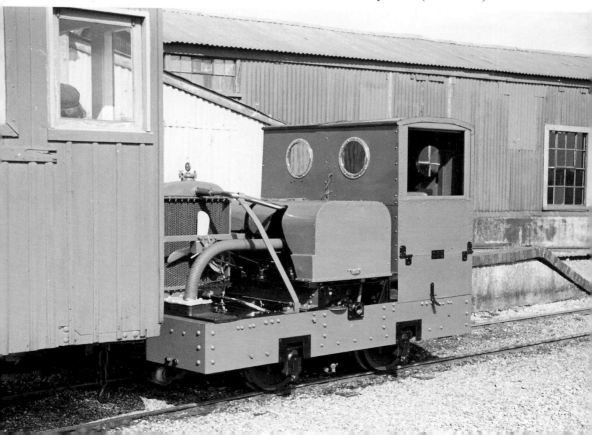

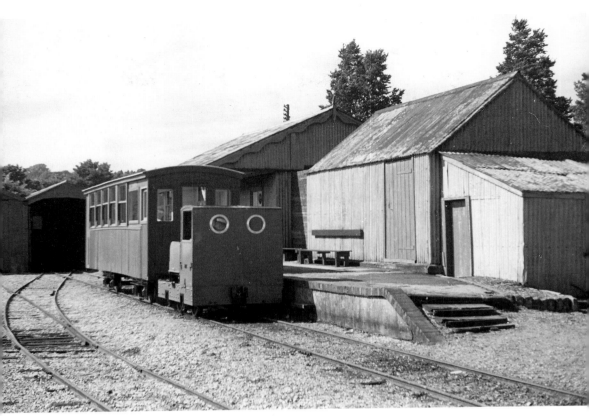

100.   The locomotive shed extension is evident in this view; it was used for carriage storage. The large shed was for coal. In the early years there was a parcels service and the charge included the ferry fee and delivery to any address in Rye Harbour. The line closed to the public on the first day of World War II, 4th September 1939, but the station was not demolished until 1947. (S.W.Baker)

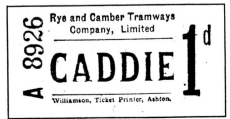

Rye & Camber Tramways Company, Limited.

FIRST CLASS.

Single Fare 6d.

3880

Rye and Camber Tramways Company, Limited.

SECOND CLASS.

Single Fare 4d.

13384

Rye and Camber Tramways Company, Limited

A 8926

CADDIE 1d

Williamson, Ticket Printer, Ashton.

Rye and Camber Tramways Company, Limited

A 0984

Third Single

Sands
Child

2d

Williamson, Ticket Printer, Ashton.

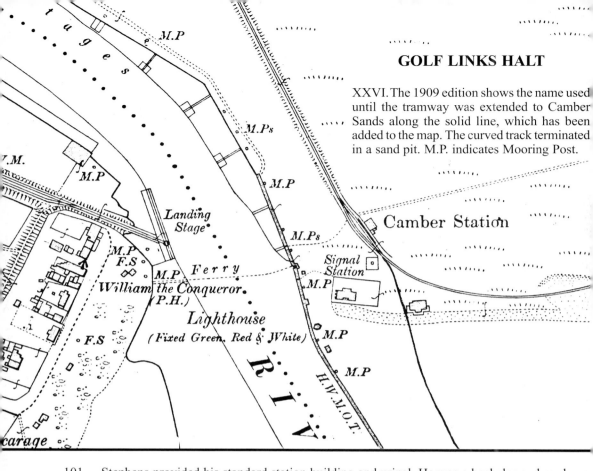

GOLF LINKS HALT

XXVI. The 1909 edition shows the name used until the tramway was extended to Camber Sands along the solid line, which has been added to the map. The curved track terminated in a sand pit. M.P. indicates Mooring Post.

Labels on map:

M.P

M.Ps

M.P

M.P

Camber Station

Landing Stage

M.Ps

Signal Station

M.P

M.P

F.S

William the Conqueror (P.H.)

Ferry

Lighthouse (Fixed Green, Red & White)

F.S

R I V ...

H.W.M.O.T.

M.P

M.P

caraqe

101.   Stephens provided his standard station building and urinal. He was a bachelor and made no provision for ladies. The sandy nature of the terrain is evident and was presumably used by them. (Unknown)

102.   A photograph from 12th July 1931 suggests that the loop had been removed sometime earlier, although it was shown on the 1929 Ordnance Survey. Rye Golf Club generated the main traffic in the early years and even subsidised the tramway in the 1914-25 period. (H.C.Casserley)

103.   The tramway was abandoned during the early part of World War II and the village of Camber was evacuated, due to fears of invasion. The line was requisitioned by the Navy in the early part of 1943 to link a training establishment set up near the Rye terminus with the harbour. The loop was reinstated, a branch (left) to a pier was laid down and concrete was poured around the track for the benefit of road vehicles. (S.C.Nash)

104.   Another photograph from April 1946 shows the pier, which was built as part of the D-Day invasion preparations, albeit a very small part. The tramway was used by the Navy until about May 1944; this included transport of shingle from the southern terminus. (S.C.Nash)

105.   The building survived the war intact (the one at Rye was used by the Navy as the Guard Room). It came into the care of Rye Golf Club for use as a store and its future thus seems assured. The photo is from February 1995, by which time the awning area had been infilled. (V.Mitchell)

CAMBER SANDS

106.   One of the tramway's two open four-wheeled coaches is included in this August 1929 view. There were two gaps in the far side for access, but no doors. The chassis of the Bagnall coach (right) eventually found its way to the Amberley Museum. (Unknown)

107.   No shelter was provided for passengers and all tickets were issued by the guard, or driver latterly. Included in this August 1938 panorama is the tea hut, which later became a pig sty. (R.S.Carpenter coll.)

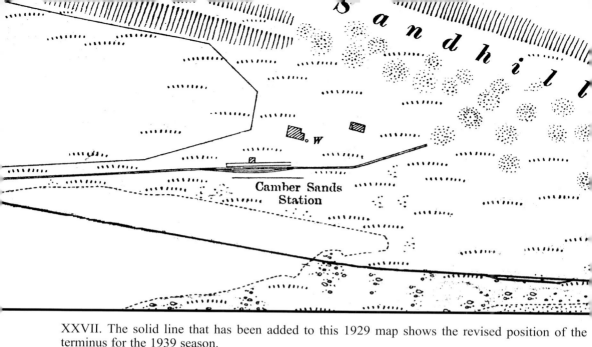

XXVII. The solid line that has been added to this 1929 map shows the revised position of the terminus for the 1939 season.

108.   The new platform (and bench) was in use from 6th April 1939 until 3rd September of that year. Its close proximity to the beach meant that shingle could be loaded easily. Several reporters remarked upon the driver's informal dress, but then it was largely a holidaymaker's line by then, golfers having deserted it in favour of road transport. (S.W.Baker)

VOLKS ELECTRIC RAILWAY

	DEPOT	
UARIUM	PASTON PLACE	BLACK ROCK

XXVIII. Route diagram in 2001. For details of operating times, please telephone 01273 292718.

AQUARIUM

109.   Britains first public electric railway was opened at noon on 4th August 1883 and ran between the Aquarium (left of the camera) and the Chain Pier, which was in the right background until December 1896. The line was extended from there to Paston Place on 4th April 1884, dipping steeply to pass under the pier. Much of the route was on a timber viaduct after 1894, which was subject to storm damage. Previously it had been on the beach. For the first season the gauge was two feet and it was 2ft 9ins for a brief period, but 2ft 8½ins was employed subsequently. One of the early short cars is passing through sea spray in the Edwardian period.   (D.Smith coll.)

110.   A new western terminus was opened at the Aquarium on 27th June 1930, the section to the Palace Pier being sacrificed for road widening. It is seen in 1938, five years after the 50th anniversary of the railway's opening. It had been built on land leased from Brighton Corporation who acquired

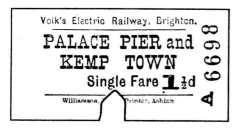

the concern in 1939, but retained the name of its designer and builder. This building was destroyed during World War II and was replaced by a former tram shelter, shown in the next picture. (D.Smith coll.)

111. For about the first three years, the running rails were used as electrical conductors, but subsequently a third offset rail has been used, with current return via the other rails. The beach can be seen under the track in this 1973 view - the line was closed for most of World War II. Only one platform has been used since the mid-1960s, since which time most cars have run in pairs. (E.Wilmshurst)

Brighton Corporation Transport
Volk's Electric Railway

AQUARIUM
TO
BLACK ROCK
Single Fare - - 3d

Williamson, Ticket Printer, Ashton-under-Lyne

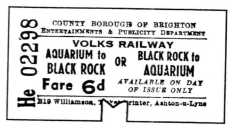

COUNTY BOROUGH OF BRIGHTON
ENTERTAINMENTS & PUBLICITY DEPARTMENT

VOLKS RAILWAY
AQUARIUM to
BLACK ROCK OR BLACK ROCK to
AQUARIUM

Fare 6d   AVAILABLE ON DAY
OF ISSUE ONLY

B19 Williamson, Ticket Printer, Ashton-u-Lyne

PASTON PLACE

112.   This station ceased to be a terminus named Kemp Town in 1901, when the service was extended to Black Rock. Since that year cars have run through the shed in which storage could be increased by removing the platform! On the right is the 1930 all-weather car, numbered 5. For a few years around 1900, it was possible to change here to the "sea-going" tram on long legs for a trip to Rottingdean. Photographs are included in *Brighton's Tramways* - Middleton Press. (D.Smith coll.)

113.   The portable platform was replaced in 1947 by an island one, west of the shed, but cars still ran through the latter. This view from May 1949 includes both car sheds, the railway's office and workshops are above the word PETER. There is no rail connection to the latter, although there was in the early days. (S.W.Baker)

114.   Car 2 (now restored to its original no. 9) is westbound on 4th May 1952 and is crossing the path to the Banjo Groyne, prior to passing through the shed. The driver has his left hand on the controller, a curious location that was perpetuated until 1963. The section of track in the background is on a viaduct, but it has vanished under shingle. (J.H.Moss)

115.   On 8th August 1999, the southern shed contained an ex-Southend Pier Tramway toastrack car, one of two 1899 Falcon cars purchased in 1949 and numbered 8 and 9. The works train is powered by a diesel built by Alan Keef Ltd in 1987. (V.Mitchell)

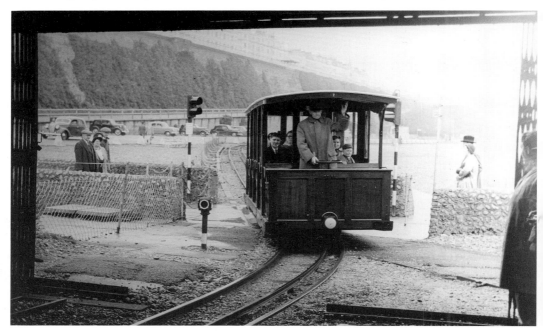

116.   The alternative names for the station are shown at the end of the platform as the newly qualified lady driver waits to depart east on 7th May 2000. Car 6 has the two-tone livery adopted in 1962. The station was named "Lift" for some of the early years. (P.G.Barnes)

117.   With his right hand in the revised controller position, the driver of car 4 of 1892 leaves the eastern loop on 23rd April 1987. The line did not run regularly in the Winter after 1954. Cars 6-8 date from 1901, 9 from 1910 and 10 from 1926. (P.Groom)

Fb 9965

Volk's Electric Railway

AQUARIUM

TO

PASTON PLACE

Fare **2d**

Williamson, Ticket Printer, Ashton-u-Lyne

B 9586

BRIGHTON CORPORATION TRANSPORT

VOLKS RAILWAY

BLACK ROCK *to*

CHILDREN'S PLAYGROUND

CHILD under 14

Fare **2d**

AVAILABLE ON DAY OF ISSUE ONLY

Williamson, Ticket Printer, Ashton-u-Lyne

BLACK ROCK

118.   The eastern terminus is in Kemp Town and was used by many local residents throughout the year in the early days. Initially only this hut was provided at this station. (D.Smith coll.)

119.   More spacious accommodation was provided in 1911, no doubt welcome at this often windswept location. This was followed by a further new building, which was opened on 7th May 1937 when the route was shortened slightly to 1.1 miles. (D.Smith coll.)

120.   A new terminus was opened in 1948 and it is seen on 4th June 1950, as crowds wait to travel and a full car arrives. The railway had closed on 2nd July 1940, due to the threat of invasion, and it reopened on 15th May 1948. (J.H.Moss)

121.   The station was given a fresh name, Marina, in 1979 as a massive new marina had been built nearby. It was so large that a supermarket was built on some of the unused space. This October 1994 view includes the surface site for contractors creating a storm water storage facility, using one of the Channel Tunnel boring machines. A temporary terminus was provided to the right of the crane for four years. (J.H.Meredith)

122.   The fifth terminus was recorded on 7th May 2000, the platform having been built adjacent to the new pumphouse of Southern Water. It opened in 1998, but there was no weather protection for passengers. Hopefully, Brighton will have councillors in the future who appreciate this jewel in the nation's narrow gauge crown. (P.G.Barnes)

Volk's Electric Railway
BLACK ROCK
TO
AQUARIUM
Single Fare **3d**
Williamson, Ti Printer, Ashton-u-Lyne
Ug 9061

BRIGHTON ELECTRIC RAILWAY
One Adult or One Child
For ONE JOURNEY ONLY
Not available for
DAY Excursionists
This Ticket must be presented
for cancelling and collection
Williamson, Ticket Printer, Ashton
Rf 9826

Middleton Press

Easebourne Lane, Midhurst, W Sussex. GU29 9AZ Tel: 01730 813169 Fax: 01730 812601
If books are not available from your local transport stockist, order direct with cheque,
Visa or Mastercard, post free UK.